One Season Behind

Books by Sarah Rosenblatt

On the Waterbed They Sank to Their Own Levels
One Season Behind

One Season Behind

SARAH ROSENBLATT

DRAWINGS BY SUZANNE ROSENBLATT

CARNEGIE MELLON UNIVERSITY PRESS
PITTSBURGH 2007

Acknowledgments

Grateful acknowledgment is made to editors of the following periodicals in which some of these poems first appeared:

Free Verse: "Pangs" and "About Death"
The Clark Street Review: "Mornings at Starbucks" and
    "An Allegiance"
Philadelphia Poets: "Two Months After Luc's Death"
Poetry Harbor: "Fall"
Confrontation: "Sentry Foods on Downer Avenue"

I would like to thank my mother for the beautiful drawings. My father for his unconditional support. And Craig for all his help, support and editing. Thanks again to Gerald Costanzo, without whom this book wouldn't be possible. Thank you to Cindy Pawelski. Thank you to Tracy Wabyick for her insightful editorial input.

Publication of this book is supported by a grant from the Pennsylvania Council on the Arts.

Library of Congress Catalog Control Number: 2006922785
ISBN 13: 978-0-88748-466-7
ISBN 10: 0-88748-466-2

10 9 8 7 6 5 4 3 2 1

PENNSYLVANIA
COUNCIL
ON THE
ARTS
40th Anniversary

Contents

OUTSIDE OUR INFLUENCE

For my parents, my brothers, and Craig, Cal, and Jake

One Season Behind

Packing Them In

The lunches I pack each day
start out fresh and wholesome
and days later,
stink.

Summers become progressively warmer
and the doormat picks up
the bottoms of our feet
the way autumn does
ending the free-for-alls in the avenues.

My son asks, "Does Santa bring the years?"
I say, "I'm not sure what brings the years."
He says, "Maybe space."

Look Both Ways

Things happen outside our realm of influence.
Presidents are re-elected,
the Chinese New Year blows by.

A day well-spent is taken over by night.
It has the upper hand,
scrubs the kitchen of its colors.

Our children look up to us
as if what we say goes . . .
but where?

The patio smells of supper from the night before.

Afternoon blasts the bedspread.
Why are we here?

What was the reason given to us when we were small,
starting out in classrooms
where each of us was the center of something?

Now our children ride bikes,
look both ways
parade into day.

Deflections

We're all in this together—
a throng of us
preparing meals,
smiling at strangers,
realigning our cars.
All moving forward
with a surety.

But then an uneasy tone
rings in the trees
with an alacrity that undercuts the sunshine
on our faces.

We begin to travel
as if to avoid something.

When we were younger
we wondered how
we would handle middle age.

Now, years later,
we catch glimpses of it in others
before we recognize it in ourselves.

Living the Way We Do

The sun didn't shine again. As usual most people were living
by the seats of their pants.
Nights were clear and stars still made their point.
Sneezes were under no one's jurisdiction . . .

Subsisting as we do
without enough time to finish each gesture,
life's important questions are put aside again.

Meanwhile, the architecture builds around us
and we have little to say about what is put up.
The changes in the terrain are incorporated quietly.

No one keeps tabs on the night light
or just how many shadows
are in the kitchen
when the orange streetlights shine through
the lace curtains.

One Season Behind

The coming together
of two people
in the middle of a house,
their middles touching.

The trees outside
mingle with the plants inside.
Light comes through the screens
and swirls into the hairs on the cat's back.

Here they are—the summer at its height—
yet they feel like they are just beginning to poke through,
as if most of July hadn't just blown in
and out of the trees and the mouths of the cats
asleep in the red chairs.

Under the ceiling fans
summer doesn't take shape
until the red and orange leaves
give them a jump-start
on the flavor of lemonade.

Fall

They eat under umbrellas at the lake,
their follow-throughs in sync with the water.

Summer tilts off the leaves
and fall comes in with a frankness
that meets the clothing head on.

There are changes in the skyline
and in the patterns of boats on the lake.

A new phrase
that had been mouthed around for months
now wraps up
on the horizon.

That era slips into this one.

The Moment

We lived out the whole day in anticipation of the next—
as if one slot of time was worthy of overrunning another.

Saturday was enjoyable, free-floating.
But now the memory competes with Sunday evening
blue-purple over the lake.

Groups of teenagers walk with the darkness.
We are all walking
on the threshold of something.

The fragrance of the lilacs booms into the night.
We sneeze differently
but the atmosphere takes it in the same way.

7/26/92 S.Rosenblott

Digging In

We eat, drink,
linger over our scones
in such a way
that no one
can inflict anything on us today.

October maps out its territory
on the sides of our eyes—
forgiving itself for not being more
than it is.

No one springs anything on anyone today.

And no one makes complete statements about the birds
and their whereabouts.

7/05

Two Months After Luc's Death

The sun shines through a tall man's ears,
making them glow.
Children watch the garbage truck
through holes in the wire fence.

The morning passes
through the child's sifter in the sandbox,
and through the households
immersed in ritual.

A child touches the birthmarks
on his father's back,
saying, "Sun, moon, sun."

The summer moves forward
with picnics
and questions

retrace themselves in the bones of my fingers.

From Year to Year

Everything came and flowed
and went away and returned.
And turned and dreamt
and woke and returned.
And slept and ate
and drank and returned.
And flipped sideways over fences,
over sidewalks, over grass.
And rolled over through fields
and swished around
and pulled back
and returned and returned.

The Love in the House

8/28/93

Undressing for the Seasons

We had the house—the beautiful house—
although the shutters were at loose ends.

He camped out in his invoice
and touched the underpart of my arm.
Someone had said, "Relax, let it happen as it will
in due time, with the climate of change
in your bellybutton."

It was still warm—
people were standing out on corners
wearing pink and purple.

The leaves carried the sky out over the grocery
where a well-built man unloaded
a Tradewind's pizza truck
with yellow gloves in summer.

Pregnant for Fall

There's only a mild crunch of summer
in our Caesar salads
as we anticipate fall in the sky,
a bit further up,
with a touch more darkness.

This was the beginning of something
too big to put a finger on.

Although I assumed myself distinct,
my body would go through
what other women's bodies go through.

Pangs

Breathing is something that,
like taking care of our children,
comes naturally,
as does daylight
entering the bedroom
dropping rainbows on the walls.

You love them so much
they stab at your innards
even now that they are out,
bathing dinosaurs.

Something about their eyelashes
and their questions
lashing out,
like scythes into a field of corn.

My Son Cal at Sixteen Months

Today I watched you scoot across the floor
to see the prism
hanging in the window.

Later we read stories,
pulled laundry baskets over our heads,
looked at each other through the ribs.

Tonight as you sleep
I listen to your breathing

as the placemats in the dark kitchen hold their own
throughout the Fall,

supporting the living
the best they can.

Where We're Meant to Be

This is the house
where we belong.
This is how the doors
are meant to swing,
where our elbows rest,
where we slip
into the cushions.

Love is something we sink into . . .

My deceased dog flutters mysteriously
in the corner of my eye.

It's the little accidents
that riddle us
forever.

Beware of Season

The morning rolling over on itself,
like us in bed.
We did what we could
but were unable to get over
the hump—
winter
hanging on
in the backyard
rounding the trees
barking at us
as if we were strangers approaching the house.

Airing Ourselves

It is a day like others—
swallowing us
as we go about our business
crunching numbers.

Daylight stabs the integers.
The laundry exacts itself in the wind.

The Catskills grin at us
from behind the trees,
letting us know this day *is*
no matter what our view.

Heat Rising

It is hot
and everyone
(even those with a high tolerance
for change)
welcomes sleep.

The moon shines through fans
leaving networks of shadows
on bare backs.

Mothers lose
the reverberations
of their words
in the backyards.

Urban Voyeur

The seven o'clock light pushes through the window
into the tiny kitchen,
catches the steam rising from the red pots
and the loose hair and glasses
of a tall woman in purple, washing asparagus, their tips
glowing.

She holds up a paper bag.
Its thin surface turns bright yellow.

It's a small two-room apartment
with a turtle swimming in a circular bowl,
a statue of a tall, thin bird on the table,
a wooden sculpture of a man fishing in her bedroom.

Our Upbeat Children

Our upbeat children
gallop on the floorboards.

Later, at school,
our insiders
are in the masses.

It hurts to see them dissed by others,
although we know they have
the wherewithal to withstand it,

love lining their coats.

Manic Spring

Finally a bit of spring in the air
and in your feet. The charms around your neck
tap dance.

You are chock-full of hope
with this new reference point
that fully involves
all your body.

To breathe in the vastness of it
is overwhelming.

An expansiveness
stretches across your face—
your smile threatens
to become out of sync with the horizon.

The Love in the House

Driving my cat home
from the hospital—one leg less—
I sing, "Sometimes I wonder if I'm
ever gonna make it home again"
in my grandmother's voice.

I am myself
but with the hinges
of my ancestors.

The love in our house keeps us loyal,
but the snow comes down
without heed for us
piling on our brows.

The changes are beyond us
as are our own natures,
staking us out in the afternoon.

Each Generation Advancing

Just when middle age was the great beyond
you wake up in the face of it.

Those younger than you filter into coffee shops
and onto roadways,
putting you in your place.

Somehow your peers have adapted.
They smile as they march past the grocery
and summer slips into the ends of their hair.

An Allegiance

My grandma—a black sheep—
married a black sheep.
Together they created others,
with a flare for irreverence.

We came here on their coattails.
They brought us
then opted out.

We continue on,
procreate,
bleat out our genetic take
on the universe.

The universe sniffs at us
then forgets our scent
as it moves to the next tree.

It's Difficult to Imagine

It's difficult to imagine
my mother and father
sucking their pacifiers and
sleeping away their first months.

Then establishing themselves
on two feet and
grabbing lamps.

Later, going out into the community
and, at school, coming to grips
with the realization that discoveries
made at home in the limelight
were not as impressive
to a crowd of peers.

At the Bottom of My Stomach

Sadness drops in
like an old friend.
She is lovely and entirely delicate,
so sensitive that I
my marriage
my children
may wreak havoc on her,
may keep her up at night.

Outside Our Influence

Feeding the Ducks

I'm anticipating a time when we can waddle,
shake water off tail feathers,
zoom across ponds
under gulls and red and orange leaves
that hang
like anything that hangs,
falling insubstantial,
above in the air.
Like anything that shuffles above our heads
or in our heads—
the simple talk of anything in particular
that falls together as easily as words
then breaks apart on top of water
after words are said,
rippling under the ducks that move.
And that is all.

Chandeliers hang above
people at a party
whose heads
are orange, white and brown

and insubstantial like leaves
that fall off in the wind
and sink into water
down, down, down,
and fizzle under ducks,
under anything that moves.

Suzanne Rosenblatt -'03

Rooting

Two boys build castles.
Clouds skedaddle northward.
So many hotels. So many remarks
taken at face value.
The afternoon stomps through the afterthoughts and
the bird feet impressions in the sand.

At night waves hit the shore
like teeth colliding in the mouth
of a sleeping child.

Suzanne Rosenblatt 12/01/96

Not Minding

Mothers watch closely
as their children romp
in the lake.
The horizon
shirks its responsibilities.

A couple runs in the wet sand,
their reflection rips through the puddles.

Sunbathers read the sunlight
on their closed lids
taking the summer for what it is.

An Israeli City

The loose paint on the bedroom ceiling
was an Israeli city from above—
the white roofs of the Jews, the red roofs of the Arabs.

We slept
then woke in the night
belly to belly.

It was unsettling to think
that so much animosity
could have built up in the navels
of people
who roll around in the dust
together.

Outgrowing Our Homeland Security

This leader had always had more than enough,
like certain girls in grade school
who acted as if they had an edge
on the rest of us.

In the café a homeless woman
turns from person to person
asking if he or she
is angry with her.

A well-kept woman
waits for her coffee,
looks straight ahead—
not intending to face
up to anyone's gaze.

On Their Own

The willingness to go through years with a partner
and be with him
so many years later
entering a café
with cloudy windows
and the smell of the familiar,
yet a new conversation develops—
between two
whose features became distinct
from their parents
years ago.

Mornings at Starbucks

The regulars, who had known how things were,
were becoming shakier,
less sure of their words.

They came each day
as if congregating
would make the story clearer,
less impatient to move on.

A well-built man parks his bike outside.
His face is red—
not beyond the elements.

He orders coffee
and drinks it slowly,
tries to hang on.

Miami Beach—
The Elderly Once Owned the Avenues

In polka-dotted tee shirts,
they shuffled past mint green hotels.
Their bellies overhung their shorts.
Their lifelines sunk inward.

Any reassuring pat was welcomed
by their backs,
remembered there.

Side by side,
their eyes registered the tides
that left imprints
of spines in the sand.

About Death

How limited we are
even once we've decided
we want to stay.

Dreaming about it
I wake in the night—

sinking
in my birthmarks . . .

until the tables clank
with the morning people.
They express themselves day in and day out
with a confidence
that makes me feel at home.

Married to the Outside

We walked.
The sun brightened our noses,
cloaking all divisions.

We married,
but your sense that all was outside
kept you with the masses
at bands and festivals
with people in shorts.

You met the afternoons
without a center.

I left.
What else could I do?

Sentry Foods on Downer Avenue

Shoppers pass the grocery.
My grandmother used to wander this street
in her red coat,
unsure of where she was,
fearful someone might notice.

She never admitted to vulnerability,
breathing it in
and compressing it.

When she slept
the wind insisted
on rounding off her features.

Piracy

Friends and family eat
in the aftermath.
The future takes us
as we are
with our hair
our noses
entirely themselves.

Our son plays with his pirate ship in the tub,
saying, "I'm alive. I'm alive. I'm alive."
He likes the warm water,
the froth of never-never land.

Previous Titles in the Carnegie Mellon Poetry Series: 1995-2007

1998
Yesterday Had a Man In It, Leslie Adrienne Miller
Definition of the Soul, John Skoyles
Dithyrambs, Richard Katrovas
Postal Routes, Elizabeth Kirschner
The Blue Salvages, Wayne Dodd
The Joy Addict, James Harms
Clemency and Other Poems, Colette Inez
Scattering the Ashes, Jeff Friedman
Sacred Conversations, Peter Cooley
Life Among the Trolls, Maura Stanton

1999
Justice, Caroline Finkelstein
Edge of House, Dzvinia Orlowsky
A Thousand Friends of Rain: New and Selected Poems, 1976-1998,
    Kim Stafford
The Devil's Child, Fleda Brown Jackson
World as Dictionary, Jesse Lee Kercheval
Vereda Tropical, Ricardo Pau-Llosa
The Museum of the Revolution, Angela Ball
Our Master Plan, Dara Weir

2000
Small Boat with Oars of Different Size, Thom Ward
Post Meridian, Mary Ruefle
Hierarchies of Rue, Roger Sauls
Constant Longing, Dennis Sampson
Mortal Education, Joyce Peseroff
How Things Are, James Richardson
Years Later, Gregory Djanikian
On the Waterbed They Sank to Their Own Levels, Sarah Rosenblatt
Blue Jesus, Jim Daniels
Winter Morning Walks: 100 Postcards to Jim Harrison, Ted Kooser

2001

The Deepest Part of the River, Mekeel McBride
The Origin of Green, T. Alan Broughton
Day Moon, Jon Anderson
Glacier Wine, Maura Stanton
Earthly, Michael McFee
Lovers in the Used World, Gillian Conoley
Sex Lives of the Poor and Obscure, David Schloss
Voyages in English, Dara Wier
Quarters, James Harms
Mastodon, 80% Complete, Jonathan Johnson
Ten Thousand Good Mornings, James Reiss
The World's Last Night, Margot Schilpp

2002

Astronaut, Brian Henry
Among the Musk Ox People, Mary Ruefle
What it Wasn't, Laura Kasischke
The Finger Bone, Kevin Prufer
The Late World, Arthur Smith
Slow Risen Among the Smoke Trees, Elizabeth Kirschner
Keeping Time, Suzanne Cleary
From the Book of Changes, Stephen Tapscott

2003

Imitation of Life, Allison Joseph
A Place Made of Starlight, Peter Cooley
The Mastery Impulse, Ricardo Pau-Llosa
Except for One Obscene Brushstroke, Dzvinia Orlowsky
Taking Down the Angel, Jeff Friedman
Casino of the Sun, Jerry Williams
Trouble, Mary Baine Campbell
Lives of Water, John Hoppenthaler

2004
Freeways and Aqueducts, James Harms
Tristimania, Mary Ruefle
Prague Winter, Richard Katrovas
Venus Examines Her Breast, Maureen Seaton
Trains in Winter, Jay Meek
The Women Who Loved Elvis All Their Lives, Fleda Brown
The Chronic Liar Buys a Canary, Elizabeth Edwards
Various Orbits, Thom Ward

2005
Laws of My Nature, Margot Schilpp
Things I Can't Tell You, Michael Dennis Browne
Renovation, Jeffrey Thomson
Sleeping Woman, Herbert Scott
Blindsight, Carol Hamilton
Fallen from a Chariot, Kevin Prufer
Needlegrass, Dennis Sampson
Bent to the Earth, Blas Manuel De Luna

2006
Burn the Field, Amy Beeder
Dog Star Delicatessen: New and Selected Poems 1979-2006,
       Mekeel McBride
The Sadness of Others, Hayan Charara
A Grammar to Waking, Nancy Eimers
Shinemaster, Michael McFee
Eastern Mountain Time, Joyce Peseroff
Dragging the Lake, Robert Thomas

2007

So I Will Till the Ground, Gregory Djanikian
Trick Pear, Suzanne Cleary
Indeed I Was Pleased With the World, Mary Ruefle
The Situation, John Skoyles
One Season Behind, Sarah Rosenblatt
The Playhouse Near Dark, Elizabeth Holmes
Drift and Pulse, Kathleen Halme
Black Threads, Jeff Friedman
On the Vanishing of Large Creatures, Susan Hutton